STEM
SUPERSTAR
WOMEN

GRACE
HOPPER

Advancing Computer Science

Megan Borgert-Spaniol

Checkerboard
Library

An Imprint of Abdo Publishing
abdopublishing.com

abdopublishing.com

Published by Abdo Publishing, a division of ABDO, PO Box 398166, Minneapolis, Minnesota 55439. Copyright © 2018 by Abdo Consulting Group, Inc. International copyrights reserved in all countries. No part of this book may be reproduced in any form without written permission from the publisher. Checkerboard Library™ is a trademark and logo of Abdo Publishing.

Printed in the United States of America, North Mankato, Minnesota
102017
012018

 **THIS BOOK CONTAINS RECYCLED MATERIALS**

Design: Emily O'Malley, Mighty Media, Inc.
Production: Mighty Media, Inc.
Editor: Liz Salzmann
Cover Photograph: AP Images
Interior Photographs: Alamy, pp. 10, 20; AP Images, pp. 9, 25; Harvard University Archives, p. 16; iStockphoto, pp. 7, 27, 28 (right), 29 (left); National Archives and Records Administration, p. 23; Shutterstock, p. 28 (left); Wikimedia Commons, pp. 5, 13, 15, 19, 29 (right)

Publisher's Cataloging-in-Publication Data

Names: Borgert-Spaniol, Megan, author.
Title: Grace Hopper: advancing computer science / by Megan Borgert-Spaniol.
Other titles: Advancing computer science
Description: Minneapolis, Minnesota : Abdo Publishing, 2018. | Series: STEM superstar women | Includes online resources and index.
Identifiers: LCCN 2017944046 | ISBN 9781532112805 (lib.bdg.) | ISBN 9781532150524 (ebook)
Subjects: LCSH: Hopper, Grace Murray, 1906-1992--Juvenile literature. | Women computer engineers--
United States--Juvenile literature. | Women admirals--Juvenile literature.
Classification: DDC 510.92 [B]--dc23
LC record available at https://lccn.loc.gov/2017944046

CONTENTS

//

GRACE HOPPER

Mathematician Grace Hopper found her calling during **World War II**. As a member of the US Navy Reserve, she **programmed** computers for use in national defense. Later, Hopper invented the first computer programming language that used English words. She then helped lead the effort to establish a universal computer language.

Throughout her career, Hopper often **predicted** the future of computers. She believed that computers would be useful to everyone, not just mathematicians. She imagined computers in offices and homes. At the time, many people thought Hopper's predictions impossible.

> **"Humans are allergic to change. They love to say, 'We've always done it this way.' I try to fight that."**
>
> –Grace Hopper

Grace Hopper's nickname in the navy was Amazing Grace. Her colleagues greatly admired her skills and witty personality!

But Hopper was committed to **innovation**. On a wall, she hung a clock with hands that moved backwards. The clock taught a valuable lesson. It was a reminder not to be held back by the way things have been done so far. Hopper lived by this lesson. She knew that innovation was only limited by one's ability to imagine it.

2

A CURIOUS CHILD

Grace Brewster Murray was born on December 9, 1906, in New York City. She was the oldest of three children. Grace's younger **siblings** were Mary and Roger.

Grace grew up in a time when girls were not commonly encouraged to pursue **academic** careers. But Grace's parents, Mary and Walter Murray, thought differently. Mary wanted her daughters to have academic opportunities that she didn't. Walter wanted his daughters to go to college so they could support themselves as adults.

Mary and Walter encouraged Grace and her siblings to be curious. Grace took a special interest in learning how things worked. At seven years old, she took apart seven alarm clocks in the family's home. She was trying to figure out how the alarm clocks rang!

Grace attended schools that also encouraged curiosity. They taught her to think and to rely on herself. In 1924,

Grace was accepted at Vassar College in Poughkeepsie, New York. That fall, she took the train to the city to begin her college career.

Vassar College was the first university in the United States that granted degrees to women. It now admits both men and women.

3

FROM STUDENT TO TEACHER

//

At Vassar, Murray was eager to learn as much as she could. She studied mainly mathematics and **physics**. However, she also attended classes in geology, economics, and other subjects.

Murray also discovered a talent for teaching. She once **tutored** another student who was failing physics. She helped that student earn a passing grade. After this success, Murray began tutoring more students in physics. She became known for her ability to clearly explain difficult ideas.

In 1928, Murray graduated from Vassar with a **bachelor's degree** in mathematics and physics. She then continued her studies at Yale University in New Haven, Connecticut. In 1930, she earned a master's degree in mathematics from Yale.

Hopper received more than 40 honorary degrees from various universities.

Hopper was an inspirational teacher and her classes were very popular with students at Vassar.

That same year, Murray married Vincent Hopper and took his last name. She had accepted a teaching position at Vassar, so the two settled in Poughkeepsie. At Vassar, Hopper taught several different math classes. While teaching, she also continued her own studies. In 1934, Hopper received her **PhD** in mathematics from Yale.

At Vassar, Hopper became known for her unusual teaching methods. She once had her students write essays about a mathematical **formula**. Many of the students complained that they were not there to learn English. Hopper responded that their knowledge was useless if they couldn't communicate it to others.

Hopper continued her own education while she taught. As a teacher there, she could attend classes at Vassar as well. She loved to learn about subjects outside her own field. Hopper took courses in astronomy, biology, and more.

During this time, Hopper began to see that every subject has its own language and symbols. Hopper thought about how mathematics could be used in different fields of study. Hopper began to see that it could be used to help solve problems of all kinds.

4

DETERMINED TO SERVE

Hopper taught at Vassar into the early 1940s. In 1941, she and Vincent separated. That same year, Japanese planes dropped bombs on Pearl Harbor, a naval base in Hawaii. The United States entered **World War II** soon after.

Like many Americans at the time, Hopper wanted to help with the war effort. In 1942, the US Navy established a women's reserve. Hopper tried to join. However, she was not accepted right away. Her main obstacle was that the navy had a weight requirement. Hopper did not weigh enough to **enlist**.

WORLD WAR II WAVES

Hopper was admitted into the navy reserve as a member of WAVES. This stood for Women Accepted for Volunteer Emergency Service. The women in WAVES did navy jobs on shore so more men could fight in the war.

By the end of World War II, more than 84,000 women served in the Women Accepted for Volunteer Emergency Service (WAVES) program.

Hopper wouldn't take no for an answer. She requested that the navy lift the weight requirement for her. In 1943, the navy granted her request and agreed to let her **enlist**. Hopper was sworn into the US Navy Reserve.

5
MEETING MARK I

In 1944, the navy assigned Hopper to the Bureau of Ship Computation Project at Harvard University in Massachusetts. She would be working with the first **programmable** computer in the United States. The computer was called Mark I. It was 51 feet (16 m) wide and 8 feet (2 m) tall!

Hopper's job was to program the computer to perform mathematical calculations. Hopper worked under Howard Aiken, the designer of Mark I. Aiken was a tough commander who demanded quick work. Hopper had never programmed a computer before. Aiken gave her just one week to learn how to program Mark I.

Programming the Mark I required giving it instructions for each operation. First, Hopper and her team translated a mathematical problem into a code that Mark I could understand. Then, they entered the coded problem into the computer using paper tape with holes punched out.

The Mark I was designed in 1937. It was operational from 1944 to 1959.

Hopper considered Howard Aiken (*left*) an excellent leader who challenged his colleagues each day.

Mark I did important calculations for the navy during the war. These calculations helped gunners and rockets hit their targets. The calculations also helped locate and remove magnetic mines that could blow up passing ships.

After **World War II** ended in 1945, Hopper remained in the navy reserve. She was made lieutenant in 1946. Hopper also decided to stay at Harvard as a researcher.

Hopper continued to work with Mark I. One of her projects was writing a book about Mark I and how it worked. Hopper's book was the world's first computer **programming** manual. Hopper also helped develop Mark II and Mark III. These computers worked at increasingly faster speeds.

Hopper's research position at Harvard ended in 1949. It was time for her to find new work. Hopper did not want to return to teaching mathematics. She was too interested in computers. So, Hopper entered the commercial computer business.

6

UNIVAC AND FLOW-MATIC

In 1949, Hopper joined Eckert-Mauchly Computer Corporation (EMCC) in Philadelphia, Pennsylvania. The company was working on the Universal **Automatic** Computer, or UNIVAC. Hopper was in charge of **programming** the UNIVAC.

As she worked on the UNIVAC, Hopper began to explore how to simplify computer programming. At the time, programmers had to enter long strings of 0s and 1s to instruct computers. These number strings were called binary code.

Hopper and her team developed a method of storing common binary codes in the UNIVAC. Then they assigned

THE MIGHTY UNIVAC

The UNIVAC was the world's first commercially produced electronic digital computer. It ran a thousand times faster than Mark I!

call numbers to each code. This way, **programmers** writing new programs could include these common codes without reentering long strings of binary code. All they had to do was enter the call numbers. The computer would do the rest of the work.

In 1952, the UNIVAC successfully predicted the results of the US presidential election!

Hopper is considered the main person behind the success of COBOL. She persistently promoted COBOL to the military and businesses.

Hopper completed this new system in 1952. She called it the A-0 compiler. Improved **versions** were called A-1 and A-2 compilers. The A-2 compiler was released a few years later. This was the first compiler to be used by many **programmers**.

Still, Hopper believed **programming** could be simpler yet. She imagined a computer program that was written with words instead of mathematical symbols. So, Hopper programmed the UNIVAC to translate letters into computer code. She called this system the B-0 compiler.

In 1958, B-0 was released under the name FLOW-MATIC. Now, programmers could write commands in English instead of binary code. This made programming possible for people who were not mathematicians.

The FLOW-MATIC compiler only worked on UNIVAC computers. Other computer manufacturers had their own languages. In 1959, Hopper helped assemble a committee to develop a universal computer programming language. They came up with the Common Business-Oriented Language (COBOL). Over the next ten years, COBOL became the preferred programming language for business.

7

CALLED BACK TO DUTY

During her time in the commercial computer business, Hopper continued to serve her country. She did so as a consultant and lecturer for the US Navy Reserve. In 1966, Hopper had to retire because of the navy's age limit. Later, she said the day she retired was the saddest day of her life.

However, a few months after she retired, the navy asked her to come back. The navy had begun to use COBOL and was having problems with it. There was more than one **version** of the **software**, and they didn't all work with each of the navy's computers. The military needed Hopper's computer **programming** expertise once again.

Hopper took a leave of absence from EMCC, which had become Sperry Rand Corporation. In August 1967, she reported for temporary active duty. Her orders were to help set up standards for COBOL software so it could be used on all the navy's computers.

Hopper continued to lecture at various universities. She thought one of her greatest accomplishments was training young people.

Hopper's temporary active duty lasted nearly 20 years. Under her direction, the navy standardized COBOL and produced a manual for using the **software**. Hopper also gave lectures at universities, businesses, and **technology** events. She encouraged everybody to take an interest in the future of computers.

8

THE OLDEST OFFICER

Hopper's military career came to its official end in August 1986. She had achieved the rank of rear admiral the previous year. Hundreds gathered for her retirement ceremony aboard the USS *Constitution* in Massachusetts. This was longest-serving ship in the Navy. And at 79 years old, Hopper was the oldest officer on active naval duty.

During the ceremony, Hopper received the Defense Distinguished Service Medal for her contributions to national defense. She would later receive the National Medal of **Technology** in 1991. The National Medal of Technology is presented to individuals or groups that have strengthened the United States through technology. Hopper was the first woman to receive the medal as an individual.

Hopper continued to work after she retired from the navy. She became a senior consultant at a computer

Hopper served in the navy for 43 years. She was also one of the first women to receive the rank rear admiral.

After her death, Grace Hopper's spirit lived on in the **software** industry. In the early 1990s, women **programmers** at Microsoft formed a support group. Group members called themselves the Hoppers. The group addressed the **discrimination** against women. It also discussed how to increase the number of women working in computer software. Around the same time, Hopper's **legacy** inspired the Grace Hopper Celebration of Women in Computing. Today, this annual conference is the world's largest gathering of women in computing.

company called Digital Equipment Corporation. She also traveled the country giving lectures on the future of computing. On January 1, 1992, Hopper died at her home in Arlington, Virginia. She was 85 years old.

Since her death, Hopper continues to be recognized as a computer science pioneer. In 1994, she entered the National Women's Hall of Fame. In 1997, a new navy ship was named USS *Hopper*. And in 2016, President Barack Obama awarded her the Presidential Medal of Freedom. These honors celebrate Hopper's commitment to **innovation**. They celebrate a woman who kept her eye on the future and never looked back.

Hopper was buried with full military honors in Arlington National Cemetery.

TIMELINE

1906

Grace Brewster Murray is born on December 9 in New York City.

1928

Murray graduates from Vassar with a bachelor's degree in mathematics and physics.

1934

Hopper receives her PhD in mathematics from Yale University.

1944

Hopper is assigned to help program the Mark I computer at Harvard University.

1949

Hopper joins Eckert-Mauchly Computer Corporation (EMCC) in Philadelphia. Her job is to program the UNIVAC.

1958

Hopper's B-O compiler is released under the name FLOW-MATIC. It is the first English-language compiler.

1959

Hopper helps lead a committee that develops COBOL, a common programming language for businesses.

1967

Hopper reports to the US Navy for temporary active duty. Her assignment is to help standardize COBOL software.

1986

Hopper retires from the navy. She receives the Defense Distinguished Service Medal for her contributions to national defense.

1992

Hopper dies on January 1 at her home in Arlington, Virginia, at the age of 85.

GLOSSARY

academic—relating to school or education.

automatic—moving or acting by itself.

bachelor's degree—a degree that is earned at a college or university, usually after four years of study.

discrimination (dihs-krih-muh-NAY-shuhn)—unfair treatment, often based on race, religion, or gender.

enlist—to join the armed forces voluntarily.

formula—a mathematical fact or rule expressed in letters and symbols.

innovation—a new idea, method, or device.

legacy—something important or meaningful handed down from previous generations or from the past.

payroll—the money paid by a company to its employees.

PhD—doctor of philosophy. Usually, this is the highest degree a student can earn in a subject.

physics—a science that studies matter and energy and how they interact.

predict—to guess something ahead of time on the basis of observation, experience, or reasoning. Such a guess is a prediction.

program—a set of instructions or commands for a computer to follow. Someone who writes or inputs a program is a programmer. A device that can be programmed is programmable.

sibling—a brother or a sister.

software—the written programs used to operate a computer.

technology—the use of science in solving problems.

tutor—to teach a student privately.

version—a different form or type of an original.

World War II—from 1939 to 1945, fought in Europe, Asia, and Africa. Great Britain, France, the United States, the Soviet Union, and their allies were on one side. Germany, Italy, Japan, and their allies were on the other side.

ONLINE RESOURCES

Booklinks
NONFICTION NETWORK
FREE! ONLINE NONFICTION RESOURCES

To learn more about Grace Hopper, visit **abdobooklinks.com**. These links are routinely monitored and updated to provide the most current information available.

INDEX